Joseph Nguyen is a spiritual thought leader who has a mission of helping others realize their divine purpose, unlock the infinite potential of their own mind, and live an abundant life, free from psychological suffering. He spends most of his time writing, coaching, teaching, speaking, and sharing timeless wisdom to help people discover their own divinity from within, and how they themselves are the answer they've been looking for, throughout their lives.

Nguyen is also the author of the #1 international bestseller *Don't Believe Everything You Think,* which has been translated into over 31 languages, worldwide.

beyond thoughts

an exploration of who we
are beyond our minds

joseph nguyen

AMARYLLIS

AMARYLLIS

An imprint of Manjul Publishing House Pvt. Ltd.
• C-16, Sector 3, Noida, Uttar Pradesh 201301, India
Website: www.manjulindia.com

Registered Office:
• 2nd Floor, Usha Preet Complex,
42, Malviya Nagar, Bhopal 462 003 - India

Distribution Centres
Ahmedabad, Bengaluru, Chennai, Hyderabad,
Kochi, Kolkata, Mumbai, Noida, Pune

Original English language edition published by Joseph Nguyen,
Florida, USA.
Arranged via Licensor's Agent: DropCap Inc.

This edition first published in India in 2023
Fifth impression 2025

ISBN 978-93-5543-235-3

Printed and bound in India by Thomson Press (India) Ltd.

for Kenna, my divine muse who shows me a love beyond words each day

contents

beyond the surface

as above, so below

it is tiring trying to manipulate the world
to match our expectations of it
and we wonder why
most of us are exhausted all the time

when i let go of my expectations
of who i want you to be
i can finally see
the beauty
of who you are
and set us both *free*

judgement blinds us
from seeing
who we truly are

(blind spot)

i'm confined
by what i compare myself to

(the cages we create)

every judgment we make about others
is one we've already made
about ourselves first

(as without, so within)

frustration cannot exist without expectation

give people the grace
to be where and who they are
          without wishing they were different

letting someone be who they are
          does not mean
you have to be any less than your true self

(unconditional acceptance)

if the world is a reflection of who we are
why am i trying to change the image i see

instead of me?

(the illusion)

what if the reason we hurt
comes from judging what's better or worse?
why can't things just be different
          and that be enough?

what season in nature is right or wrong?
what if our differences could be the reason we
          feel like we belong?

(beyond judgement)

everything is perfect…

when i don't judge it

(perfection is)

why can't we see that we're two sides
    of the same coin?
two leaves of the same branch?
two waves in the same ocean?
two notes on the same scale?
two souls connected to the same source?

(the illusion of separation)

the world is a reflection of us

what we hate about ourselves
　　　　is what we hate in others
what we love about ourselves
　　　　is what we love in others

everything external
　　　　comes from the internal

what we do for ourselves
we do for the world

(the great mirror)

it takes a painful amount of energy
to try to be someone else
instead of yourself

what we hold on to
holds us back

self-care
is the most selfless
thing you can do

what if your commentary about life
is getting in the way
of you actually *experiencing* it?

(reality needs no commentary)

most of us are chasing external things
so that we can feel something inside
innocently forgetting that all feelings
are generated within us

what is external
is only a reminder
that we can create
the internal emotion we desire

what you most want to experience
can only be found within you

don't wait for something outside of you
to give you permission
to feel how you want inside

(don't wait for permission)

growing up we learned
that silencing our voice
  is music to everyone else's ears

and now our minds
have become a deafening orchestra of
  opinions
that have dominion
  over our own

(silence ≠ peace)

the voice inside your head
　　　might *sound* like yours
but have you ever stopped to realize
most of the words
　　　are from someone else's mind?

(inception)

break the vicious cycle of attachment and
suffering by asking yourself this:

are you focusing your attention on fully and
unapologetically expressing yourself

or on external outcomes?

(are you in or out?)

most of the advice
we received in our childhood
was focused on worrying
about what others think
instead of expressing ourselves
and how we feel

give yourself the permission
which you weren't given growing up

how people treat you
is a reflection of how they treat themselves

this goes both ways

(third law of e-motion)

you're not unhappy
because you don't have the approval of others
but because you've lost yourself
in the process of seeking theirs over your own

(lost and found)

for every lie
        there is a seed of truth
for every truth
        there is a seed of untruth

if i despise you
        it's because you remind me
of a part of myself i don't want to see

behind every mask
        is a truth we're afraid to face

instead of waging wars to determine who's
        right and wrong
why can't we accept that each of us is both
        and get along?

what's true is never in the extremes
        but somewhere in between

we are not problems needing to be solved
but humans needing to feel heard and seen

(yin-yang)

the world doesn't exist to make us happy
it exists to help us realize our own power
that we can be happy
          no matter what happens in it

(resilience)

what if life isn't a game
          you can win or lose
but more like a song
          and you are the muse?

(you are life's masterpiece)

you are not here to be accepted
you are here to be the exception

who am i?

who am i
if the thoughts in my mind
aren't mine?

(who am i)

just like how a cloud
    is not the sky
we are not the thoughts in our minds
    but the space inside

(s p a c e)

i am not who you think i am
i am not even who i think i am

(beyond identity)

where do thoughts come from?

why are we so attached
to what does not come from us?

daily reminder:

you are what is beyond your conditions and circumstances

wholeness and feeling enough
aren't things you attain
but something for you to realize
is your true nature

(you are what you seek)

when you become aware
that you don't need to be fixed
        because you're not broken
all illusions that aren't actually you
begin to d
i
s
s
o
l
v
e

(if it ain't broke…)

when you don't mind
what's inside your mind
you'll be surprised
at how much peace you find

(no mind)

never forget that what you do and create
is *part* of who you are
but not who you are

hope

what is it going to take
for you to see that you're not a mistake
but an *indispensable* part of the world
that can't be replaced?

(irreplaceable)

one of the greatest powers we possess is *choice*

gratitude is acceptance of what is

hope is understanding nothing lasts
forever

peace is being unattached to
what is in the mind

you'll know you're healing
when you can find the beauty in pain

(signs of healing)

do you have faith
that you will survive
what you fear most?

when the world around you
        seems overwhelmingly chaotic
remember that you can always
        find the eye of the storm

peace is when you realize
        you are the eye

(you are the "I")

beyond thoughts and thinking

thoughts are inevitable
thinking about them is unnecessary

it is not thoughts that cause our suffering
but our own thinking about them

(thoughts vs. thinking)

thoughts are inherently neutral
thinking is the act of thinking
    about our thoughts

when we think about our thoughts
we cast our own conditioning, judgements,
    and story onto the thought

we can't control our thoughts
but we can control if we think about them

and if thinking is the root cause
    of our own suffering
then we can control
    whether we suffer or not

(the root cause of our suffering)

what emotion do you feel
        when you're not thinking?

this is the secret
        to unconditional joy and peace

(beyond thinking)

i think, therefore i suffer

you become the thoughts you are attached to
but You are not your thoughts

when you let go of what you think
you discover who you truly are

our natural state is peace, love, and joy, but we've been conditioned out of it through thinking. without thinking (the act of thinking about our thoughts instead of just allowing thoughts to pass unencumbered), we return to the state in which we came into this world.

food that your body doesn't let go of
        causes indigestion

thoughts that your mind doesn't let go of
        causes anxiety

(when we don't let go)

thoughts are transient
they come and go
        but **You** always stay

if you want to know who you are
look beyond your thoughts
to experience your true nature

(the only constant)

you don't have to think
in order to know

questioning your own thinking creates

s p a c e

for new thoughts
to change your life

an object in motion will stay in motion unless acted upon by an external force. questions are one of the greatest external forces that can stop negative thinking because it acts as an external force that interrupts the pattern of thinking and creates space in your mind for new ideas that it didn't have before.

if you don't ask yourself a question
you don't know the answer to
you'll keep thinking
        the same thing indefinitely

new questions
        lead to new answers

powerful questions to help you stop negative thinking:

is every thought in my head true?

is this thought serving me?

what's the cost of believing this thought?

what emotion would i feel when i let this thought go?

thinking creates the illusion of duality
the past and future
that things are good or bad
right or wrong
and that all things are separate from you

without thinking
the illusion falls apart
you come back into the present moment
and you realize that everything not only
comes from the same source

but *is* the same source

(oneness)

the absence of thinking (self)
is the presence of peace (divine)

you are not what you think
you are not your thoughts

just like how you are not your hand
but that you *have* a hand
you are not your thoughts
you *have* thoughts

you are what is beyond your thoughts

(the great beyond)

beyond fear

have you ever noticed
behind what you fear
is what you want most?

(fear is the path)

fear and desire
  are two sides of the same coin

is what you're thinking
keeping you alive

or preventing you from living?

ambiguity breeds anxiety
specificity creates clarity

you are not your fears
but the space that holds it
you have the strength already within you
to do what you fear most
            when you let go of your thinking

are you making decisions

to feel safe

or to feel *free*?

anxiety and fear only come from our minds
trying to use the past to predict the future

the mind cannot comprehend the unknown
but our hearts can trust it

the unknown is the only space
that contains new possibilities for your life

(the unknown is home)

the point is not to attempt to become fearless
but to not be afraid of the feeling of fear
so that you can truly live a life of freedom
from mind

(the myth of fearlessness)

to the person who is okay
with the feeling of fear
the whole Universe yields

you're not afraid of what you think you're
afraid of

you're not afraid of what could happen

you're afraid of how you'll **feel** *if* it happens

what we think is an external battle
is really a civil war

(the war within)

the way to overcome fear
is to become aware
of what you're afraid of feeling

(the way out)

fear is a mirror
into the parts of ourselves
we have yet to bring to light

(illumination)

the world would feel a lot less scary
if we admitted we all are afraid

when you look at your deepest fears
what are you afraid of happening most?

do you notice how you're more afraid of what
other people will say
and what you'll say to yourself
rather than the actual event?

do you notice how what you would say about
yourself if what you feared most happens

is the same thing you're already
saying about yourself now?

(fear: the greatest revealer)

living an abundant life
comes from following your fears
          instead of letting them control you

become curious about your fears
for they are the doorway to your dreams

if you don't have the courage
to face the music
you'll never get to hear
the most beautiful melodies
life has in store for us

(the symphony beyond ourselves)

courage is not the absence of fear
but the presence of love
in the midst of fear

letting go

what we hold on to
perpetuates our reality

what we let go of
creates new possibilities

(the end is the beginning)

transformation is not a result to be achieved
but a byproduct of letting go
to be *experienced*

(evolution is inevitable)

how long are you going to keep holding on
to the story you don't want to keep reliving?

what you resist, persists
what you let be
    will inevitably leave

(the natural course)

the path to self-actualization
isn't to try to improve ourselves
          because we think we're not enough
but to let go of the illusion
that we're not already enough as we are

(awakening)

can you forgive yourself
for doing the best you could
with what you had?

if you knew better
          you would have done better

it's time to free yourself
          from the prison of the past
                    and the fear of the future

(self-forgiveness)

intuition

miracles live in the land of intuition

do you want to feel confined
by listening to the mind?

or do you want to feel alive
by following your intuition?

the fruits of following our intuition
always seem miraculous
and even impossible
to those who don't

if you want to attract abundance into your life
follow what feels expansive and unknown

this is what your intuition feels like

you can never know what to expect
when following your intuition
but it is *predictably miraculous* every time

intuition speaks to us in the present
without worrying about the past or future

because it knows it is creating both

(the language of intuition)

beyond duality

the only use of these words
are to put your mind to sleep
so your soul can speak

(beyond words)

an empty mind is a peaceful heart

without conscious intention
we default to our conditioning

when you focus on external outcomes
you sacrifice your internal happiness

without expectation
for how things should be

there is no longer frustration
with how things are

life isn't fair
it is balanced

emotions are an invitation
into the present moment

how often are we avoiding our emotions
and therefore

the present?

(you're always invited)

live your life
like watching a movie

where you're not stressed out
trying to figure it all out
but enjoying the experience
of what's happening in front of you right now
        no matter what happens in it

(the observer)

you don't have to try so hard
to change or grow
because everything
is always doing so

it is a law of nature

the reason why it's so difficult to change
isn't because we're not trying hard enough
it's because we are afraid
          of what might happen if we do

what if you holding onto what got you to
where you were yesterday

is the reason you can't get to where you want
to go today?

(attached to the past)

success and failure
are nothing more
than what you think it is

whether you feel like you're one or the other
is determined by your definition of them

(confined by our design)

one of the most important choices
you make each day
is choosing to be
the creator of your life

or the reactor
        of what happens in it

(creator vs. reactor)

what would happen if you didn't treat
other people's opinions as facts
and everything you think as truth?

(what if?)

true freedom
isn't in having complete control of our minds
but in the ability to be unattached
to what happens in it

(true freedom)

a quiet mind
is the soil
from which serenity sprouts from

(source of serenity)

how helpful is the voice
that narrates and comments
on everything in your life?

what would happen
if you stopped treating that chatter as truth?

(auditing the inner critic)

you cannot think your way into flow
just as much as you cannot think your way
    into love

both are a natural occurrence
when we let go
and allow the full authentic expression of
    yourself to come forth

they are a byproduct
    of surrender and trust

(falling into faith)

joy doesn't come from what you do
but from the *energy* and *intention*
behind what you do

happiness is a byproduct
of bringing a sense of playfulness
to everything you do

(joy is not a result)

everything is energy
energy is everything

sometimes all we need is a friend
to confirm we're not as crazy
as we think we are

letting your light shine brighter
does not dim anyone else's
it only gives them permission to do the same

(light is abundant)

the way to step into the beauty
        of who you are
is by letting go
        of who you think you need to be

(beauty is)

when we have the courage
to go into the unknown
we discover what we need to know

(possibility awaits)

most of us only change
when the pain of holding on to what we're
attached to
is greater than the fear of the unknown

(rock bottom)

we've been conditioned
to be serious
when our natural essence
is *playfulness*

what we are attached to controls us
what we are unattached to liberates us

what you think becomes your reality

let go of what you think
and your reality changes

when you let go of your thinking
you naturally enter the state of flow

let go to enter flow

(flow)

where your attention goes
energy flows
where energy flows
things grow

what are you growing?

(the gardener)

what we all are searching for
and wanting in life
are things that money cannot buy
and what we cannot hold in our hands

(beyond the physical)

a closed mind suffers
an open mind experiences peace

success is not what you accomplish externally
but how you feel internally

what you find within yourself
    can never be taken away from you

(the truth)

we tend to overestimate
    the power of our actions
and underestimate the impact
    of our presence on the world

the path to peace
is through letting go
of what we think we know

the more you unlearn
the more peace
and joy you'll earn

if you want to stay alive
nourish your body

if you want to feel alive
nourish your soul

(soul food)

the laws of the spiritual are much different than the laws of the physical. when you give something spiritual like love, you do not have less of it, but more. the spiritual is always abundant and infinite. we are no different.

we tend to overvalue things we pay for
and undervalue the gifts in life that are free

(life is a gift)

be cautious of making an absolute conclusion on how you think about something. when we determine something is absolute when it is truly not, we suffer.

life begins
the moment you stop fearing
your own mind

the Universe speaks
in a language foreign to most of us…

silence

(the language of the Universe)

desire without attachment
is the ultimate state of attraction

an intelligent person is constantly learning
a wise person is always unlearning

a simple way to change your life:

pay attention
to what you pay attention to

we are born creators, not consumers
to find more fulfillment in life
create more than you consume

if you're waiting for certainty
you'll be waiting for eternity

care deeply about others
but not what they think of you

a mind full of thinking
is a heart full of anxiety

the ultimate state of abundance
is the desire to continually grow
without being attached to outcomes

we are human beings
not human thinkings

if you want to be happier
think less
          and be more

if you had unlimited money, already traveled the world, had no fear, and didn't receive any recognition for what you did, what would you do or what would you create?

go do that now

(your soul's desire)

what we do not question
controls us

what we question
frees us

there's no greater gift
you can give to the world
than living in yours

(the greatest gift)

the end of another beginning

although this is the end of the book, it is just another beginning of an infinite discovery process of the unknown and who you are beyond your own thinking.

i wanted to express my deepest gratitude for you embarking on this exploration with me.

i sincerely hope you have been able to see and experience yourself in ways you haven't before and that you continue to do so each day.

if this book has resonated with you in any way, it would be an honor and a privilege to hear about your experience.

the best way to do that would be to leave a review on amazon so that it can reach many wonderful souls who are also looking for the same thing you have found within yourself through this book.

what you share has the potential to transform countless lives because almost every person reads reviews before purchasing a book. i read every single one and i truly look forward to hearing about your thoughts, insights, and journey.

if you would like more from me, I have written another book titled *Don't Believe Everything You Think*, which is available on Amazon. you can find any other books I've written by searching my name on Amazon.

you may also visit my website at www.josephnguyen.org for additional resources, my youtube channel and other works i've created.

for any other inquiries, you may email me a info@josephnguyen.org.

with love,
joseph

acknowledgments

i wanted to take a moment to thank my mentors and teachers that greatly inspired this book such as sydney banks, michael neill, and joe bailey. through them, i have discovered many of these ideas in the book that were already within me (and in each of us) to be able to share them with you here.

a special thank you to my beautiful fiancée, kenna, who patiently and graciously grounds me in the present moment every day through unconditional love. it is because of you that i have been able to find myself.

thank you to my family, friends, and each person i've come into contact with as you all have been wonderfully supportive in my journey of discovering the truth within myself and for encouraging me to share it with others so they can find theirs.

you all have my eternal gratitude.

The other bestselling books by Joseph Nguyen published by Manjul Publishing House

THE SPACE WE CREATE WITHIN OURSELVES

Our emotional suffering does not come from the events in our lives, but from how we respond to them. Each boundary we set helps to create space for a different behaviour and response when we are faced with the same situation that causes our suffering. The space we create within ourselves is the source of infinite possibilities for us to choose peace and a new experience of life.

ALTHOUGH PAIN IS INEVITABLE, SUFFERING IS OPTIONAL.

Don't Believe Everything You Think offers a completely new paradigm and understanding of where our human experience comes from, allowing us to end our own suffering and create how we want to feel at any moment.